Plain Prose and Poetry

Vivian Laster

iUniverse, Inc.
New York Bloomington

Plain Prose and Poetry

Copyright © 2008 by Vivian Laster

All rights reserved. No part of this book may be used or reproduced by any means, graphic, electronic, or mechanical, including photocopying, recording, taping or by any information storage retrieval system without the written permission of the publisher except in the case of brief quotations embodied in critical articles and reviews.

iUniverse books may be ordered through booksellers or by contacting:

iUniverse
1663 Liberty Drive
Bloomington, IN 47403
www.iuniverse.com
1-800-Authors (1-800-288-4677)

Because of the dynamic nature of the Internet, any Web addresses or links contained in this book may have changed since publication and may no longer be valid. The views expressed in this work are solely those of the author and do not necessarily reflect the views of the publisher, and the publisher hereby disclaims any responsibility for them.

ISBN: 978-0-595-53070-0 (pbk)
ISBN: 978-0-595-63124-7 (ebk)

Printed in the United States of America

A thing of beauty can be a thought planted in the mind. A thought that he or she can return to from time to time placing a smile on their faces. This is my way of contributing something to the world. I am a firm believer in the fact that a thing of beauty is a joy forever. A special thanks to all that encouraged me to complete this undertaking. My mother Velma Dillingham, William and Jerel Toliver, Khamelle, Derrick and Kimer Laster.

Contents

Indian Legend	1
Spring Forth Spring	2
Wonder Land	3
Plum Baby Talk	4
Sparks Fly	5
A Vessel that Holds the Sun	6
Dawn	7
Hold Still the Night	8
Keeper of the Ark	9
Road Runner	10
An Ice Cream Cone	11
This Violent Earth	12
Who Are They	13
To See His Face	14
Live Life to the Fullest	15
Construction Worker	16
A Place Well Found	17
Between Two Worlds	18
Love Takes a Back Seat	19
The Question	20
Circus	21
In the Dark	23
On a Bench in the Mall	24
A Point Well Taken	26
Flame	27
War	28
Under A Glass Dome	29
Ghetto	30
Snow	31
Do You Think	32
The Long Ride Home	33
Water Bug	34
Not Enough	35
Ocean Floor	36
Stop the Train	37

Lesson	38
Red Button Shoes	39
Mother	40
One Freedom	41
Child	42
The Watcher	43
Power Source	44
Tired	45
Ancient	46
External Soul	47
Informed	48
Snuggles	49
Deamers	50
The Snob	51
Butter Fly	52
Why	53
The Returning Soldier	54
Down Under	55
Atone	56
The Thing	57
Two Dogs Fighting	58
Desert Sand	59
Midnight Summers Breeze	60
No Love Lost	61
Summers Day	62
Can You Hear	63
Take the Bull by the Horn	64
Open the Door	65
Foot Steps	66
The Spirit of Fear	67
The American	68
School Time	69
Love for Lovers Sake	70
Tweet-Tweet	71
No Friend At All	72
Never Alone	73
Pityful	74

The Plight	75
Bill and Tommy	76
The Wind Blows	77
Oil Lamp	78
Mellow Street	79
On a Clear Night	80
Which Witch	81
The time is Near	82
Toy	83
Yellow Rose	84
Tabby	85
Cool of the Day	86
If Tears Fall	87
Don't Ride the High Horse	88
Good Fortune	89
Devil or Angel	90
Leaves	91
Autum and Love	92

Indian Legend

The son of a chief stood silently by, Somberly watching the maidens shy, Dark tressess fly, as she danced, Sanee caught his eye. They set the snare invaded the lair of small game and grouse and cack. Though Autummals halo came touched the blushing leaves and the tumble weeds, carpeted the earth for their feet. He had out witted the deer, buffalo, bear. And at council, fires won acclaim. Like a jewel, was she in her wedding best with tints of berries on her checks. White was the color of her buck skin dress, white was the bound of her happiness. Warriors came from the north that day, two braves they sent and spirited away the chiefs son, on his wedding day, and returning him after he was old and gray.

Spring Forth Spring

I await all good things to come , pasative things. When you arrive all things are in harmony. When you arrive all things come, alive. The air a promise of good things, to come. And we know without a doubt, spring has sprung. The mind reaches out for summer, when the birds can be heard conversing in the trees. The smell of the air says things will soon bloom, blossoms. The days are longer, the light is stronger, the sun beams pennatrate the day. The lilacs bloom and puts forth her sweet fragrance, that delights us. Spring forth spring, you have a fragrance of your own.

Wonder Land

There is a place some only dream of yet, it is every day life, for them, it enables them to be in love with life itself. The very air that surrounds wonder land has an air of promise, saying we are never doubtful, anything and every thing is possible. The clean life, the houses all are well planed seems they came from a wonder land, they don't look real, does any one live there? The people that live within, are they cheerful or are they silent, deadly quiet calculating, terror. Yet their world is their oyster, never wearing the same thing twice, that's their life. He who stands out side and having grown old, and wise. Stands in judgment of wonder land, but even he longs for a lightness of heart soul and mind. To weigh nothing at all being free posesing all, or nothing at all, in wonder land.

Plum Baby Talk

Plum baby talk, Now that we have learned to walk there no more, wable skipping, hopping, steady as she goes. Sure of this certain of that we wear a cocky hat, under which we think is a great deal of gravity. And after sipping and dipping, dribbing and dabbling into this and that, wining and dinning, and getting fat. The bib goes back on and we are reduced, after all to plum baby talk.

Sparks Fly

The eye is said to be the window to the soul and looking in one sees an amber eye with sparks of gold that is beautiful. In later years, we see all that the years have donated to it, red, brown, in the white of the eye. Finally the soul steps forward and the sparks fly, giving way to bluerd light, that has set the sparks free and threw the open window sparks fly, and out goes the soul and there is no waiste. The sparks will gather in another place, with the sparks in the sky.

A Vessel that Holds the Sun

Looking at my vessel, It always belonged to me it was beautiful in all. The innosens beamed from its radience like the sun and with love for all. Now evil has touched my vessel and handled it harshly. The vessel is now cracked, but not broken,it didn't look the same and threw the pain, it was stained, ashamed. Inside the vessel remained the same and when it came close to me, out came the sun and a smile appeared on the face, the eyes filled with tears and it looks to me the father. Oh, look at my vessel it has a heart of gold. it's the vessel that holds the Son.

Dawn

We walk in your twilight zone. They rarely speak of you, it is though you do not exist, having only a name, yet you never change, your soft purple and dark blue. All in all a lovely hue, nostalgic. Looking at you no one could say, is it night or is it day, for within you time can not be measured, at best it's a fleeting moment and you must be quick, to embrace it, or it will just silp away, turning night into day. And if you wake when it appears, you are lost in time. Is it night becoming day, or is it day becoming night, is it time to sleep or is it time to wake and start the day? Dawn my acenses must logic in your way. Away between night, away between day. Peacefull, Calm, Sapream Dawn.

Hold Still the Night

A dream come true that's me and you together we dance the night away, as sparks fly she says, hold still the night, suspend your flight. The soft wind blow across the floor and being close, she is aware of his touch. Scenses are highten and she is inlighten to the strenght in his arms she is gently lead, she thinks hold still the night, so she cant see day light. So that, she can remain, in love, for the sake of love, hold still the night.

Keeper of the Ark

Looking into the rising sun, to a place where time begun, there comes a murmur a wonder. What will be found under these leaves in the land of the fig trees. Is it here he asked? Yes the keeper replied, with graying hair, He dose not despair. At the intruders remarks concerning the ark. The keepers child like face, child like eyes, will not lie. This dark form is a wise priest, no sin present in the mind or body a soul that's a delight to see. The guardian of the Ark, stands tall, black, and being holy. He totally tells the truth and with no fear he turns and speaks no more. And locking the frail wooden gate, to seal, to steal as never before, the Ark. A word to the wise truth wears a disguise, there is no fear it is clear, that the Ark takes care of the keeper.

Road Runner

Road runner, feel the thunder
Here there, every where,
running the road with out a care
this they know, they are on the go
the road is there home and for know
its were they belong, singing a song.
Run road runner run
always laughing full of fun
life for you has just begun
don't take it hard, just be smart.
And play the right cards
Run road runner run,
tiered, is a word, one they never heard.
Up at dawn and they are on the way
as night becomes day
Run road runner run
don't let life use you like a dart
putting you in the place you start
don't let grass grow under your feet
Come on and join the fleet, and
Run road runner, run!

An Ice Cream Cone

To a wide eyed child of five that dressed in her Sundays best, dressed in her sun back dress. Something as simple as an ice cream cone, that wont last long, is the high light of her summers day, and just to hear her grandma say, lets get an ice cream cone. And on their way home, she savors the flavor, to the last lick, trying to make it last. A pleasure, one she will treasure, something as simple as a ice cream cone.

This Violent Earth

Burning valcanos flow into the oceans full of sharks the earth quakes make sure that the lines become clear, the winds blow strong destroying homes, can man control it all? Can man over come the world? It ahs been written, there is a way unto man that seems right. We have had miracles, And science and by employing these two methods man has tried to control, the elements, hoping to over come the terra firm, which of these two, science or miracles, are right? One way and that was Jesus' way. He over came the world, Jesus stated that he had over come the world, by working miracles, walking on water, calming the sea, making the blind to see, raising the dead, he controlled the elements and life and death, was in the power of his hands, find the teachings of Jesus that was left to his brother James, and to Peter. The ones that the pharaces stold and hie from the people, and we can control this violent earth, and threw Faith in GOD the father threw Jesus Christ, we over come.

Who Are They

I see it but I cant believe it at such a young age two years old, how can this be, are my eyes deceiving me. They said this was not possible, It had to be something learned, or taught by someone else in order for this to be, but yet, here it is, an angle walking among us. Man cant see them they have mislabled them and because of this wrong name, they act accordingly. Look at their faces, the calm, peace in thee face, it demands attention this soul that shines on the outside of the body. If you see one be slow to judge, look closer give them time to show weather they are angle or devil. If they live holy lives, than they are angels. But is they an evil perverted life, than they are devils.

To See His Face

Lord I want to see your face, has been echoed down threw the centuries. But how dose one look upon a spirit, what would we see? Can we bare to look upon the face of GOD? And see him as he really is. There is a longing, a love makes man to want to connect with his maker. Enoch pleased GOD and walked away with GOD. We have the word and with the word Jesus, we see love materialize, we are not satisfied being blind. Lord I want to see your face, we hear the sound of the mighty rushing waters our names called softly in the night, all draws us ever closer, closer to you.

Live Life to the Fullest

Live life to the fullest, change all that you can, this time remember don't forget about yourself. Live life to the fullest, tomorrow might not come, go on and have some fun, give yourself the best, but don't forget about the rest. This time live life to the fullest and have no regrets, let the sun shine in and with a good friend, this time in life, live life to the fullest.

Construction Worker

On a clear day, off in the distance they can be heard, in the wee hours. It's a bright sunny day, in the cool of the morning. She wakes to the sound of a jack hammer drilling into concrete and there is the sound of heavy equiptment moving soil here and there. These sounds to her means life is going on big things are happening, excitement, she becomes caught up in these sounds and thinks what is going up today. The old men and the young men, gather around in groups watching the workers and take about the best way to do the job. The men in hard hats are at work. She lay in her bed and wish she could watch as well close at hand, but her imagination along with the sounds will have to do for know, as she snuggles deep down in her pillow and felling secured sleeps, omn a clear day

A Place Well Found

Don't have me just any where, pick a place for me , for safety is the key. Don't leave me just any where with some one that don't have a care. Pick a place for me, a place where there is no disgrace, a clean clear place and they will love to see my face. Im the unborn, let me feel no scron, love is what I want from you. Don't leave me just any where pick a place for me , place me in the right womb, and very soon you will become me and I will become you and carry you as a memory, from one generation to the next, you become immortal. Pick a place for me, don't leave me just to fall to the ground leave mein a place well found.

Between Two Worlds

Like the mermaids of the sea, beckons to the sailors, on a balmy night, they beckon to me, there is peace here says the mother, I have a home for you here its dimly lit but its well fit. They beckon, friends all gone saying were still having fun, come. The father she once knew, who made all her dreams come true. Beckons the brother once full of life beckons from a bar stool drinking laughing, saying see nothing has changed all is the same, he beckons the uncle full of fun says life here has just brgun. He beckons the husband holds her tight in a grip of love larger than life, he holds his wife and says come, she loves them all dearly but she thinks clearly, life beckons me.

Love Takes a Back Seat

Dark, black as the blackest night and at first sight, one would think good lord, surly he is on the bottom of the heap, taking a back seat sits love, with eyes peering out from a dark face, never boosting or bragging, no complaints calm, quit. And watching something beautiful it is revealed, lying down deep. He is a feast for the eye, a joy to the soul. When he moves his strides are like the steps of a gaint. IT seems a king has been reborn and walks among us. His gaint steps landing in the grass moves the tall form smoothly, glidding from side to side in a masculine way and watching her heart skips a beat, she is aware of a gentle presents lying just beneath the surface of this person.That show threw the eyes. The dark form moves with long strides, his head held high, in the tradition of an Egypt, pride. Connfident in his present undertaking, a smile crosses his full lips that brighten his face. Now comes the light and it grabs for the dark, tearing, clawing, the way to the bottom in order to be on top of the heap, as love takes a back seat.

The Question

Dose GOD really need man? It has been said, that GOD uses man in this realm to do work for him. Because GOD is a spirt, The truth is GOD is GOD and he don't need man to do nothing for him, in this realm or any other realm.

Circus

The leaves are all falling to the ground and there's a chill in the air , as the squirrels scurry about looking for food, for the winter and sitting among tha oak trees, stood Washington park, and the big top. The main tent is brightly colored yellow, blue. The children are running with excitement, and big smiles on their faces, as their parents strain to keep up with them. The young lovers stroll along hand in hand and standing out most in the crowed are the ones in the winter of their years, heads full of gray hair recapturing their youth. Here Daniel sits in the winter of her years, a first time circus visitor four years from seventy, she sits in a strange place, alone among all stragers, she thought she would never be here. The music started and it was loud and for each act it was perfectly suited, enhancing the performance, helping to excite the crowd. The loudness she adjusted to and the show goes on. The ring master walked around the ring, a strange looking character in all white with a tall top hat, white gloves, silver and white vest, stands this black man and there is so much make up on his face he could be any one.

    He throws his head back with a smile that illuminates the entire face of this character as he introduces each act. Enter the clowns, and speaking of the clowns were clowns in every way they were precisely clowns. The tiger tamer enters he is tall and dressed in purple, and silver pants and vest with a whip, in his hand, that never touches the tiger, the tamer is a strong black man, confidence seeps from his every move, leaving Daniel to abandon her plan to crawl along the floor if the tiger got loose, she felt a great pride in the tiger tamer. There was some thing for every one, for the young lovers, was as act called ribbon in the sky, as the two people, a man and a woman hung from two long ribbons, high above the crowd, striking different posses, of amore flying seeming in the air. The sound went up from the crowd ahhh. The tight wire, the young men preparing to walk the tight wire were dressed in tight white pants and vest, there were seven in all and of a medium height and perfectly built, they danced to the beat of Latin music their bodies swaying in a suggestive way, after all was made ready and the music ended a hush came over the crowd as they stepped out on to the wire, they were stacked in a pyramid four on the bottom, than two sitting in chairs on top of the four, and the last man sitting on top the two men in the middle completing the pyramid. The seven men moved in unison until they reached the other side, there was a hush in the crowd, until this task was completed, than the roar went up from the on lookers. The contortionist, they twisted and turned their bodies into seeming impossible shapes with grace, leaving one to think their bodies were ot quite normal. The men on stilts, they were all dressed in bright colors green, yellow, red, blue purple and orange, as they walked on stilts, the stilts were eight feet tall at least giving a festive feeling to the circus. Daniel sits high up in the back of the crowd alone as the ring master approached her, the figure leans forward and shakes her hand, with that wide illuminated smile on his face. The hand shake gives Daniel an insight into the character of this ring master, he was a person with a million untold stories. And as she strolled home kicking the leaves as they fell to the ground, she thought I'll be back next year.

In the Dark

In the dark we could have stayed, he bought us to the light, and opening our eyes we received our sight. We lift up praising hands we are not ashamed, Jesus paid the price GOD's power is revealed from the mountain high reaching up to the sky. Today we need, Joy and holynes, peace of mind we find harmony with all man kind, place me as a seal upon your heart, is a place to start and with him inside we will walk in the light, because in the dark we could have stayed.

On a Bench in the Mall

She was sitting on the bench, reading a track with thee title do you know Jesus. And this was the line used by a stranger, as he spoke to her do you know Jesus he said, she replied yes and she spoke no more. He was a stranger and as a rule she didn't speak to strangers. She looked up into his face, into his eyes he continued speaking while staring off into the distance, he spoke concerning war and the thousands of men, women and children, he had killed in war. He would not look at her, for fear that he would see the shock in her eyes, little did he know there was none. He continued speaking and starting with Genesis, in the bible and ending up with Mathew, and there he picked up Jesus. She became aware that this man knew his bible. Than he began to speak of the soilders in Viet-Nam, cursing GOD and killing each other and themselves. And looking at this man standing all of six feet seven inches tall, to her he looked like a giant, his face was ancient yet there were no limes, one would think Hannibal.

Once more walked the earth, or was it Gangis Khan? When he spoke, his voice bellowed, she felt dominated by it. He had a medical condition and spoke fondly of cocain. Jesus knew about the cocain plant he said. She thought GOD made all plants, than she thought GOD do you see this man? Was it a sin to stay alive in war time. Whose fault was it, that forced this man, into war, into hell. A man married to one woman for fifty years now, he is alone and sick. As she leaves her place on the bench, she turns to him and says, softly, there is only one unforgivable sin and that is blasphemy against the Holy Spirit. And hoping this would comfort him in some way she left. And as she went, she thought, every body needs love, don't he?

A Point Well Taken

Down threw the centuries it has been taught light is the first and all has worshiped, White bright light even though at times it has been most cruel, hateful, and deceitful by nature, fasle fire. And when the dark was mentioned the words were attached to it evil, black, and black took a back seat to any and all things white, and often times love was lost, because it didn't boast, it had no complaints, agreeable in every way and assuming the title thrust upon it, dark black ugly evil, devil, a thing to be hated. There is beauty in all things, just watching the dark move with long firm strides across the sky it unveils the stars and aid us in our slumber, and a black skin often hides a pure heart, a quite love. Now comes the bright light and it grabs for the dark and takes it by force, violence, it snatches, tears and claws its way to the surface in order to be first, But the dark was first, And if there was no dark we could never, know the light.

Flame

Flame rise high, high as the sky, Flame cook fast my apple pie, any thing bad can be used for good, Just turn it around, like you should.

War

What can they do, placing of flower at the tomb, singing their long speaking, so spirit filled? And all to honor you , the dead. What will all the speaches, flowers, heart felt sorrows do for them, raise the dead? Peace comes to mind, Peace fraudulent liars all, cowards failing to act and stop a wrong war.

Under A Glass Dome

Under a glass dome constantly seeking the way home going here and there, and at times without a care walking riding, flying high above the ground as high as the sky will allow. Where dose the sky end? So, we pretend there is some thing new, under the sun, there are things to be done, accomplishments to be made. Something to fill these days, while under a glass dome, constantly seeking the way home, all else having faded all pales in the light of truth, nothing can compare and having the dome removed, we are face to face, with the inevitable, true flight into a true light.

Ghetto

Its hard to believe, that in this day and times any good things are still happening. Upon entering an old dark apartment building, an a ran down part of town. The smells of turkey cooking stuffed with dressing, pies, sweet potatos, Its Thanksgivings, and the people are happy no matter where they are found, Even in this day and time. Even in this part of town.

Snow

The snow has mysteries stored up in it, When falling to the ground soft fluffy white snow landing on the eyelids, and lingering for a second or two, than melts, it seems a blink made it vanish, falling to the ground soft, white, snow. And in the night blowing across the street and blowing across the lights it seems to turn night to day. And tucked away inside laying in the dark, in a warm bed, she feels safe, as she watches the flurries fly, in the night sky. And when the snow touches the face, it gently cares the skin falling, to the chin. A lasting memory is its mystery, a true forget me not is a lot of snow.

Do You Think

Do you think I don't see it , I see it, I know it , I feel it. The things you go threw, and when you complain its not a shame and at times your right. But do you think you love more than I? How could you think I don't care, I am aware. I made the sun to shine, and I gave a son of mine. Wen you feel the pain, and you endure the shame, remember I came. Do you think you love more than I? I suffered and I died for you.

The Long Ride Home

She sits beside her daughter, as she drives her home. The old woman thinks back to a time past of raising this person that now sits, beside her. The old womans heart becomes heavy, thinking of the nights of hide and seek, but she and her daughter emerged victoriously, from these trials the old woman eyes are becoming dim, and her needs are great, but she will not let it be known on thee long ride home, she has left a huge lovly home, in which she did not belong. The old woman has misplaced her most prizes possesion of all her teeth, this thought and the fact that she is not really wanted brings, a tear to her eye, thinking of the small room that awaits her. She wipes away the tear defying it to fall, as she sits back looking at thee trees pass by. Home is not always where the heart is on the long ride home.

Water Bug

Water bug all of two inches long, Where did you come from,you must have a home. I just want you gone , he walks towards her bed, she wishes he were dead. Closer and closer he came. Good lord she said, he stops and looks up at her as if he understood what she was saying and went on home under her bed.

Not Enough

No time there is not enough light in the day not enough time in a life, so seek there for an eternity for the miracles must be revealed unto all of us, seek my face, seek and yea shall find, knock and it will be opened unto you ask and it will be given unto you, you start a journey of a life time plug into the power. No medicine, no magic, miracles is what we need today standing on the ground floor hoping to reach the top of the mountain, books are they true? Experiment, all that is positive is true, all good things are true. Use the process of elimination and the final analysis will be revealed.

Ocean Floor

Thee water rolls in, bringing life to the sands. That water rolls out again and there you will find them. The mermainds, soft round and pink the bright light makes them think, to scurry, and hide themselves under a rock. A form not much unlike our own, ridding the under current in a place they call home. Deep deep below down on the ocean floor. Only one has been seen, she was told to stay keen, not to go to high, or she would surly die. Mermaid stay Deep, deep below down on the ocean floor, down where the sea weeds grow, down where the jelly fish glow.

Stop the Train

The train rolls in, There no one to found, Off steps the bombs, They told us to get the hell out of town, and if we stick around, there is a job for us up town, Stop the train!

Lesson

Teach, teacher, teach learning is our gain. March soldier march keeping everyone trained so they'll feel no pain keep yourselves in shape. You'll no not what it'll take bake mothers bake. A large round cake good home are what you make.

Red Button Shoes

I have a pair of shoes that I will not loose my head is down, when I walk I don't even have time to talk, I look down at my red button shoes.

Mother

Being the first to call her mother sits' her young daughter. They would sit on the back porch and resite poems to each other. I think that I shall never see a poem as lovely as a tree, bare foot boy, these they shared as the wind blew on a summers evening, as the day gives way to night , she said look, there in the sky, at the two stars there was no reason to explain, for as the summer months drew, to an end, I alone stood on the porch and repeated, I think that I shall never see a poem, as lovly as a tree.

One Freedom

The march on Washington ending with a speech, One of freedom, down threw the centuries man has echoed the sound of freedom. Yet man has taken his most precious gift, freedom and caged it up. A few have stolen others rights to be truly free they can no longer inherit the land as was men from the beginning of time. Still the cry goes up now and forever until we are free from each other's rule and finally free of the terra ferm.

Child

They live in a small world, Hidding under tables, In a house of gables. And being raised with love love is than returned. They look for protection, and not neglection, as often they receive, A child is tender consider the lender.

The Watcher

Watching she sees him sitting there, once a strong man demanding a great deal of others, destroyed and betrayed those who loved him, as she watched she sees the pain, that has taken over his body, which he tries to hide, so that his pride wont suffer a blow as well. She knows that the strenght, and the power he once had is know gone. As she watch a glimps, tells her he is know growing weaker, is it know hate she feels? Will she take her revenge? Or has her hatred of him made the complete turn and in forming a circle meet love in it's completion.

Power Source

They were all their, from the Baptist to the Buddist standing in small groups, wearing many colors, Then she came in, she had their attention emediatly. This meeting was being held to determind once and for all. What powers if any did she posses. The clouds begain to role in the sky, as the sky darkened, as she walked amoung them. They thought were in for some rain. As she walked by some turned their backs to them and others starring in defiance, with hate in there eyes.

Her expression never changed, in spite of some of the gears she received. She begain to move faster, turning, from time to time as if in a trance. The sweat begain to fall from her face, as she went faster, from her being she was radiating, total love. For all of them. Some said we don't feel anything or see anything out of the ordinary. She has no power, some said while others stood perfectly still, watching. She turned and swirled in and out of each group, saying not a word. She than dropped to the ground, completely drained, of all her energy, perhaps dead, for their were many in the groups that wished her so. Than her people appeared at her side and laying in her hand a small stone. Her eyes opened. The people in the groups begain to run and screaming, because they could feel the love she had embedded in the very air around them and they fell to the ground dead, never to be awaken again by the love they rejected, left standing was the power source.

Tired

I've seen it all, What can happen next? Not wanted, rejected, out cast. And tiered of society rule, what, if we don't play it cool. What can happen next? A bit of excitement that's the key. I don't care what they say about me. I've seen it all, so what if I fall. What can happen next? I'm tiered, I've tried, taken all in stride. So, what if I have no pride. A bit of excitement as said before, that's what I'm looking for. If it proves fatal I'll be grateful, then, What can happen next.

Ancient

I have been up on this earth it seems, for centurys, when I smell the fresh air of a summers night I recall the years gone by, of a time, when the fashions were different when the street lights were not electric, but gas lights. There are no longer carrages drawn by horses noisy hoofs, but now, there are street car's, clanking down the streets on it's silver rails. The warm night air comes in threw the unlatched screen door, I sit back in the dark and listen to the sounds that comes in, of the children, playing around a street light a memory of family and friends, now all gone only I remain, and I feel ancient.

External Soul

Glancing in the face of total innocents. Man sees what he himself cannot explain. He says to himself, abused, misused, tormented. Perhaps a beautiful soul? Than it is thought, masculine, but yet feminine, what would be seen? Without the influence of sex, kindness, above it is said that the soul, has no sex. If one knows not which one to choose, he bears a cross that is placed, perhaps on a chosen man or woman, often unable to carry. The External Soul.

Informed

One generation after the other, of whom many call grandmother now sit their lives away, hoping that some day, in some way life, will walk threw the door, and threw conversation they pick up bits and pieces of others lives, keeping them revitalized, now they never think twice of this thing they call life. One generation after the other, of whom many call grandmother, are in good cheer and remain here hearing all that life has to offer.

Snuggles

New but Ive been here a month or two, and I like to snuggle close to you. Soft, round and brownish, pink, bet you didn't know I could think. New but I've been here four months for you, I like to smile, its just my style. If there is something wrong, you've guessed it, I know how to really protest it. I like to laugh, just say peek a boo, I see you. And when the day is threw, I love to snuggle close to you.

Deamers

Time is going by seasons are changing months pass, years pass an eternity, it seems still she waits, she thinks why, does no one want her, alone she's given to day dreaming. Of people interested in only her, captivated by her beauty, she performs, singing in a manner that in her normal state she could never do. Dance with adjility, and complete confidence, holding her audience spellbound. Returning from her dreams of grandure, she stairs in the mirror and sees an ageless face, child like and hoping her heart will win in the end. She waits, she dreams.

The Snob

There aree things that you have never had, there are things that you've never seen. There are things that you don't know, but all in all we should be the same. Yet, we are quite different. I know the right way to dress myself, I'm refined in every way, gone to all the finer places, I have created the image that is totally me. All my friends, different, looking and thinking, people you couldn't talk with, I wont reach down when I'm so far up, I might fall down, I cant show you the things I've seen or teach you the things I've grown to know and give you the things I have.

Butter Fly

Emerge butterfly emerge light and airy grace the sky. A short time you'll live, time well spent. The beauty you've lent us. Emerge butterfly, emerge, gentle beauty without a sting inspireing songs for all to sing, your metamorphasis is one of beauty and beast, your flying will soon ceast, seemingly, you appeared from no where and to no where you returned and to cage you would be a shame butter fly, fly.

Why

You love me today, you don't tomorrow, this could only bring me sorrow, but never the lass if this is best why. You cant eat this you cant eat that if you did it would make you fat. But never the less if this is best why buy. Some are takers of good and givers of bad, this is never understood, but if this is best, never the less why try. If the answers are never found.. Why? Bother.

The Returning Soldier

He's changed, the wounds have changed him take a casual glance, take in a little at a time. Could one be frightened of one that has been know for many a year? It is than thought face it when it presents itself. He is less seen coming in the gate, the uniform is distinguishable now is the time, calm down the heart, there must not be a sign of fear. The door opens and the sun streams in , lighting the middle of the room, the face changed a stranger, stands before her, she sees the love, sadness, fear of rejection, in his eyes, her arms are out stretched to receive the retruning soldier.

Down Under

Down under is where they are and it seems that they will go far, down under and when they speak it sounds quite chick is it any wonder, they dominate, down under the land came from them of old and from them many a story's are told, down under. It leaves you to wonder will they steal the thunder, those browny lads from down under.

Atone

Atone, atone for the sins, you've committed, not until I'm dead he said. Atone, atone fro the errors of your ways make sure you do, while theres still days. Atone, atone for the mischief he's done hopefully while the nights still young. Atone, atone at this very minute for you'll know not , how long you will be in it.

The Thing

I'm here, I know I'm here, some form of matter I think? I see but can not feel, I'll take a from a body, I will , I will? I will! Then I'll be able to feel, the warmth of the sun, bathing my, new form, show the love threw my eyes now that I'm properly housed, will I be better off aroused? To the things that are earthly bound, or would it have been better, not to have found, the wont to feel, then I could have blown from field to field, set forth and orbited any planet. To feel is to steal, my only treasure, which is to fly like a feather, in any weather. Now that I can no longer feel, I have no need ot heal.

Two Dogs Fighting

Two dogs fighting over a bone, the only things torn is the bone, the bone has no preference, either one can win, it doesn't care. Two dogs fighting over a bone a rag, a hank of hair, one wins thee prize, and runs with the haggard, torn bone, rag, hank of hair.

Desert Sand

Cense time begain, The desert has demanded the life of many. Some have wondered out on her, and died, and most have been driven out on the desert. In the beginning they stayed on the desert for forty years. In order to cleanse a race. And today they are forced out on the desert, in order to control the growth of a race, one would ask why the desert? The blood of thee dead is readily absorbed, by the sand, and the wild life takes care of the rest, leaving not a thing for mans hands to clean up and when the sands shifts it becomes a grave digger covering the dead, bleached white bones, leaving little if any signs of what lye baking in the desert sand.

Midnight Summers Breeze

The midnight summers breeze springs gently into morn, leaving, her caught up in moments of nastalgia. To live only in this space of time, two in love, is this not parradise? To walk together alone, in the night, with the midnight summers breeze.

No Love Lost

You are over and it has all come to an halt. It seems the air is mine to breath. The sun shines on me! Each day brings to me ! A promise of a good life, my strides become sure wide, with confidence, I'm now part of the world I once hated, you are over and I have been reborn free! I hope that in our passing, I have been able to shed some light on your dim and damdable soul. Before the change came , greif rose, riding the under currents of my mind only when deep thoughts was given, to the person you really were. The side that surfaced most was cruel, soulless, you are over and there's no love lost.

Summers Day

Winter is yet upon us , but were looking forward to you with all your bright shinning hues. The smell of the morning air, coming threw the open window, the soft wind blowing threw my hair. The birds will sing softly in the early morn there is not a sound of a car horn, a little snow is on the ground, but still you have come around, soon I'll dress in a crispt white and brown,, and walk out on a summer's day.

Can You Hear

Standing close to you I can see how strong you are, standing tall all brown and all black, talking to you I use tack can you hear? Your haylo, hangs all yellow, green, and red streaming down from your head. What storys have you heard? And what stories can you tell? Standing there all tall and strong, I can tell you've been here long. Can you hear? You have the ability to endure the weather, and you haylo falls to the ground at time like a feather, can you hear? I feel you can communicate, what do you think of me, can you hear?

Take the Bull by the Horn

They love you one and all wealthy, poor. It's in the eyes, your desires. They love you one and all gaining sight into the inner you one sees a grotesk ugly soul, hidden crouched beneath the outer, shell of loving kindness, concern, will they ever learn. They love you one and all. His present conquests is removed, feeling, feeling he's gotten all there is to be had he leaves his pray in a state of nile, and moves on to the next, be it big or small, They love him one and all.

Open the Door

The pain remember the pain, or you'll be back on the road of those who love. The joy in her heart spring at the sound of the key in the door, don't show it , or you'll lose once more. A dog shows feeling of love by wagging his tail, and licking the face, still at times he is rejected. Than is all gone, vanished and he never knew, the joy that sprang in the heart at the sound of his key in the door.

Foot Steps

A path that leads to their door seeing him before he came, they were wise enough to hide. Friends was thought they were, as his mind strays to the past. Than he was greeted as if he were needed by the ones that now hide, inside so, as he turns, finally he learns, next winter he wont enter, their path. The path of the unfriendly foe, with foot steps on the snow.

The Spirit of Fear

Rising up, the body is experiencing great pressure, it is travling at the speed of light. No planes, no space ship, no machine. Passing all the planets in the solar system the rise continues, all seems well, What's that wings down there, yes wings, flying above the planet earth earth GOD I've flown above the angles. Fear than grips the heart, Than turning to hold on to something, anything, there appears an form cloud like that, supports the grip. Than floating down in the early morning dawn, into formulary surroundings, a play ground.

The American

Long have we awaited, To once more take in your beauty, the thought of your great spaciouness! Will you welcome us home, or has our change cause you to be weary of us, we dream of running threw your thicket's bare of feet, and feel the soil underneath and we can hunt the great beast. Shed the many names given us, none being true. Once more to see the splendor of the birds see the enormous pyramids towering above the desert sands. Africa! When we come home

School Time

Color bright, color gray, come light her day. A throat of cold and a running nose, she stands out in the cold. Color bright, color gray, come light her day. A small box of crayons, she desires, not the large one with the many colors. Color bright, color gray, come light her day. Heart of might, stands this child of five, barely alive. The children look at her old clothiers, with frowns on their face, she knows that she is a disgrace.

Love for Lovers Sake

How much can one love? Start and see if you can, love like me , love is endless. It's seen in the eyes of a stranger. It's heard in the sound of music. It's read in a poem. IT's all around you , In the air you breath, cling to love's sake.

Tweet-Tweet

Each day he sits in the grass and listens to me, tossing his head from side to side, so that he can see, what his ears are hearing, he comes a little closer. Tweet, tweet, I sound as much like a bird as I can, and throws in a little love, closer, and closer he comes answering the calls with tweets of his own, If only I knew what he is saying, as a matter of fact what I'm saying as well.

No Friend At All

Sitting with this back to his friend, pushed back is an old wooden chair with his feet on the wall, his friend spoke, Donna my wife, Is the only woman I'll ever love, hearing this he sought to keep his balance, in his chair, as he thought she's your wife, but she loves me and I love her. When you mentioned her name, it made my heart, yes even the very marrow in my bones, warm, my soul soars with expectations. He than think I must now control my unsteady breathing.

Never Alone

The flowers were all thrown, the crowed all gone. She returns to her huge bed and sits at the top in a drawn up position, she try's to draw up into a knot closing her eyes the greif she feels so heavy, for her lose, it seems as if her chest would cave in from the pain. She drifts off to sleep, she sees him and in his arms, she runs with as overpowering love, she embraced him, with all the love she had stored up for many a year, all was poured into this moment. She awoke knowing, she would never be alone.

Pityful

Look at him, just look at him, Emaciated, skin and bone! It wont be long, he's smiling! Happy always happy, watch him dance, adjile on his feet, there's a joy eminating from him at these happy times, GOD what a happy man, his thin dark form glides across the floor in time to the beat of the music, snapping his fingers, no time to linger. The violet side he hides, it's only there to enforce his pride, only there for show and this they all know, he's pityfull.

The Plight

The world has become our enemy, every thing we put a hand to does not proper nor gain an inch! Even our bodies, have gone against us. The flesh has weaken in every since of the word, we feel, we feel! We might as well lay out among the trees, and let the leaves cover, us up and lay we there as night turns to day and day to night mans plight? The point of no return? Will they ever learn that threw weakness comes great strenth.

Bill and Tommy

Tall and strong, standing alone, black as the black forest, truthful, not wise, baring no disguise, he sing in an unraveling voice. Rejected while young Tommys heart forever longs for the one he calls mother. He sought love from the woman of the streets, though she was pickled to the gills with cheap rotten swill, their love was envied by most, for it was pure and close, upon her death, he wepted grievous tears for her and his childhood fears. Now united with the other one he calls mother, he lost his life for an over sight, for his insurance was sought by, mother's lover. Upon learning the facts Bill got her revenge, for the wrong that had been done and upon her soft bed, Bill lover lay dead. And this is to say, that when put to the test. It's best to know what is best, nothing was said and Bill didn't dread laying her lover to rest for revenge was sweet and Tommy she now keeps company in the grave.

The Wind Blows

The wind blows softly threw the trees rustling from time to time in her leaves. The wind blows briskly mixed with rain. The next day all is bright again. The wind blows hard. In a hurricane, hope that no one deals the pain. The wind blows on a summers night, bringing relief from the morning light.

Oil Lamp

The oil lamp give off a glow and brings back, a nostalgic feeling of a time thought long forgotten, a glimps, a fleeting moment of insecurity in the mind of a confused child, but, yet there remains the feeling of protection, as well. Supplied by warmth drawn from the red, round, bellied coal stove. And with the glow of the oil lamp, she snuggles down beneath the covers and sleeps.

Mellow Street

A tune that has an unidentifiable pitch, an instrument with an unidentifiable shape. If, the wind were to blow from a cave, or from a mountain top, or from across the great waters, would they together form the pitch? To hear it is to wonder, if it were all a dream. One that words can not explain, perhaps, if I were to continue to write, than the words might form to a degree so that you could hear what I have heard. But how can words which in themselves have been defined, possibly describe the undefined. If you, dwell within the thought, the sound will one night come to you in melody sweet.

On a Clear Night

You can be standing in the sky, hanging in the dark velvety blue, giving off your bright lovely hue. The mystery of you has long existed and to some its still quite twisted. The reason as to the when or where or even the why, doesn't really matter, your pleasing to the eye. One is not satisfied to merly lye beneath you and occasionally glance up at your beauty. Lay open all your treasures, so that all can know your pleasures. And we will know you all, bright shinning stars, on a clear night.

Which Witch

Gather her here , gather her there where she'll land I know not where she's flown high and she's flown low here and there to and fro. Clinging to a broom she'll get there soon never thought she'd reach such heights, feet are fastened tight on both sides of the straw you wont believe the things she saw. Good and round the broom she picked, hands are tight around the stick, so she wont loose her grip, if she decides, to dip.

The time is Near

Pushed back in a small room, trying to be invisible, she sits, hoping they wont see, or notice her head hanging, she thinks of the animals, and how they are devoured, If there heads hang and become weak, giving off the stench of death, instead they sit erect weaving from time to time. The old woman pushes back farther into a corner of dimly lit room, knowing that soon they will drag her out and put her away, from the things she holds dear, and the time is near.

Toy

There's a certain smell about you, that says your bright shinny and new. My toy you bring me so much joy, hopping out of my bed, you're the first thing I see, come and play with me. Now you've lost your sparkle, your wheels are broken, but still there's some use for you until my toy days are threw.

Yellow Rose

Your petals are so tender and color bright yellow you seem to delicate to touch. That's why your loved so much. Around your soft petals, just at the tip, seemed, kissed in the meadow by a fairies red lips.

Tabby

Tibbity tabby tat, tat tabby creeping across the floor. With yellow eyes she's in disguise. Tibbity tabby tat, tat tabby climbing up on the door. It's to cold down on the floor. Tibbity tabbay tat, tat tabby lean not fat sits in the corner and hunches her back. Tibbty tabby tat,tat tabby thinks she's a baby she's very lazy, as she sits out by the daisies

Cool of the Day

In every way, we seek the cool of the day, In times past there was one thing that last in times of old, with many a story told. We seek the cool of day, walks in gardens a sent from a window wee find the cool air kindels found memories of morning dew, of me and you , all is regained and remains. In the cool of the day we remain the same. And like times past, with the morning dew, I'll remember you and thank you Abba, for the cool of this day.

If Tears Fall

If tears fall from your eyes they, automatically fall from mine. My heart becomes filled with your pain and I become the same as you. Hearts become one in the love of GOD. And if tears fall from your eyes, they fall from mine, and speak of love devine, the blood shed fro me makes the soul shout, with joy, and praise, for the day had come. When tears fall from your eyes they automatically, fall from mine.

Don't Ride the High Horse

Dose GOD really need man? It has been said that GOD uses us in the realm, to do work for him, and this is because GOD is a spirit. GOD is GOD, and he don't need us to do for him, in this realm or any other realm, for he is omnipresent, and the thought that he needs us, to do his work, exist in order to lead man in the direction in which he wants us to go and that is to follow him in love and in kindness to each other, GOD loves praise and for this purpose, he could use man, but it is written, If man don't praise GOD, GOD will make the stones to praise him. Omnipresent, Omnisciense Omni potense, GOD needs no one because if he feels he needs something he will create it.

Good Fortune

They live in castle gold precious gems surround them their beds sit in a enormous room, far from the window. She has no envy of them, as she sits close to a window, atop her bed, she feels the soft early morning air blowing in, embracing touching her face, she breaths deeply this GOD given, fresh air and she envies no man, for this air money cant buy, because with it comes a peace of mind, knowing GOD is saying, I love you.

Devil or Angel

I see it, but I cant believe it, at the young age of two years old how can this be, are my eyes deceiving me they said this was not possible it had to be things learned or taught by some one else in order for this to be, but yet here it is, an angel walk, among us. But man can not see them, because he has miss named them, they bear the wrong name, they act according to the name often times looking strange, their face is peaceful, demanding attention, this soul that shines on the out side of the body. If you see one be slow to judge look closer, give them time to prove weather they are Angle or Devil if they live a Holy life than they are Angels, good. But if they live an evil perverted life than they are Devil's.

Leaves

What is a tree with out its leaves, But sticks of wood standing tall a hollow hole for birds, to nest in. The leaves are her crowning glory at her very best. They gather together and swirl around in circle, it seems as if one is trying to run ahead of the other, yet all follow in turn, as the white sun shines down on the ground, and making for them a spot light, in which to dance in. Winter has arrived and introduces its fears winds to the swirling leaves soon they will become a cover being made moist by the snow. The leaves will protect and cover the grass, that awaits spring, some thing as simple as a leaf, keeps the grass alive under tones of snow until spring arrives. And when they fall to the ground and are walked upon they make a rustling sound, and provides a carpet for man to walk on of red yellow and brown. As we kick the leaves and shuffle them along, they have such an appeal they don't seem quite real, but they put a dimple in our cheeks something as simple as a leaf. They are not just for shade, they gather the warmth from the sun, for days they gather the rays, so the leaves can feed the trees.

Autum and Love

Tree of heaven, cast down your leave, that makes a carpet for a king, rustling singing under foot, Jublilant as a bird on the wing. Gentle breezes drifting by, lift the careless curl to heaven I look a sight to see, as purple shadows fold. In reminisience garden, I pause for a while and taste nostalgia sweet, I listen to the murmer of zephers soft, lulling my heart with peace. From magnolia arbor floats a melody as the nightingale, tells his tell, mid his floral palace, he sings a sad song, in his lonely mateless retreat. I'm sure his fancy will hear his call, as it floats o're top the trees, caught by the night winds still small voice and were the dawn they will meet. But no such theme, in our practical world. The heart must sigh and sigh. The love caught in the petals of a rose and tossed to the sun set sky, will fall back to the thorny patch, there to bleed and die. Or anchor itself to some lovely ELF, to temper its downward flight, Or halt between some summer dream, to nurture its warning light, Ere the glow be gone, and the magic gone, and be lost in the velvet night. And like autumn days that decline away, like Apollo, who fled from the sky, surface things like hearts of flame, no roots will take, or bloom again. Like autumn leaves my love must be, as they kiss young faces ficklely, without farewell to the sighing tree.

www.ingramcontent.com/pod-product-compliance
Lightning Source LLC
Chambersburg PA
CBHW020015050426
42450CB00005B/477